D1391411

Homemade
Muffins

Homemade
Muffins

Carol Tennant

MQP

Published by MQ Publications Limited
12 The Ivories, 6–8 Northampton Street
London N1 2HY
TEL: 020 7359 2244
FAX: 020 7359 1616
EMAIL: mail@mqpublications.com
www.mqpublications.com

ISBN 1-84072-828-0

Printed in Italy

1 3 5 7 9 0 8 6 4 2

Text and covers
are printed on 100%
recycled paper.

Contents

Introduction

Everyone loves a homemade muffin. And here you will find all the classics, as well as some new ideas to try. For some reason, muffins have a reputation for being difficult to prepare, but hopefully these recipes demonstrate that they are actually much simpler to make than a cake. Simply mix together all the dry ingredients, mix together all the wet ingredients then add the wet to the dry and mix briefly. It's even better if the batter stays a little lumpy. And baking a batch of muffins needn't be time-consuming either, as most can be assembled, baked, and ready to eat within about an hour.

Quick breads (that is, doughs risen chemically using a raising agent like baking soda rather than yeast) became popular in American cooking toward the end of the 18th century through the discovery of pearlash, a type of refined potash, that caused the production of carbon dioxide when mixed into dough. This then creates air bubbles, which cause the dough to rise during cooking. This discovery enabled the development of all sorts of new baking ideas, including muffins. We've been using baking soda instead, since about the middle of the 19th century, as it is more readily available and cheaper to produce.

Nowadays, the range of available ingredients is vast and so are the possible combinations. Here you will find muffins to satisfy every taste—from the traditional raisin bran muffin, to the more unusual honey pistachio muffin, and all manner of chocolate muffins from double chocolate chip to chocolate fudge to banana, walnut, and chocolate chip muffins.

So, try an old favorite or better still, find a new one.

Tips for Successful Muffin Making

Mixing

Most of the muffins in this book are made using the same method: mix together all the dry ingredients in one bowl, mix together the wet ingredients in another bowl or pitcher, then add the wet to the dry and mix briefly. This means that the ingredients should only be folded together until just combined. If you see a few lumps of flour lurking in your batter, so much the better. Overmixing will only serve to toughen the muffins and they will lose their lightness and their moist texture.

Because muffins are raised using baking powder, which begins acting as soon as it becomes wet, most muffins need to be baked as soon after mixing as possible, otherwise they may not rise well and they may not be as light as they should be.

Baking

Baking times are a guide only, as oven temperatures vary. The quality of the baking pan, the size of the muffins, altitude, and the temperature of the batter when it is put into the oven also affect cooking times. In all recipes, the muffins are cooked when they are risen, golden, and spring back when pressed.

Essential Ingredients

A muffin is made from flour, sugar, raising agent, fat, and liquid. Often an acidic liquid, such as yogurt or buttermilk is used. The acid in these liquids reacts with the baking powder to give a better rise, especially where other ingredients may otherwise cause the muffins to be heavy, such as wholewheat flour or oats. Flavorings can be anything, ranging from spices to fruit to chocolate to nuts—or even a combination of all four. Many of the recipes in this book can be made from pantry staples.

All ingredients must be measured out accurately with measuring spoons and cups or weighing scales. All spoon measurements are level and all eggs are medium.

Equipment

Muffin pans: these are readily available from most good cookery stores, usually with either 6 or 12 holes. All the recipes in this book make 12 muffins, unless otherwise stated. Choose pans made from a heavy metal and preferably with a nonstick lining. Alternatively, use paper muffin liners, which make removing muffins easy and washing the dishes very simple. Also available are silicone muffin molds. These are suitable for use at high temperatures and have excellent nonstick properties. Because the material bends, the muffins pop out. On the downside, they are expensive and some brands need to be put onto a baking sheet for support. Many are guaranteed for life, however, so they are certainly worth considering.

Greasing and Lining Pans

Use vegetable oil or butter for greasing. Do not use too much, however, or the muffins will fry instead of bake.

Storage

Most muffins keep well if stored in an airtight container in a cool place. As a guide, keep muffins for around 3 to 5 days.

Freezing

All the muffins in this book can be frozen, unless otherwise indicated. Do not freeze muffins that have been frosted or decorated, although these can be frozen first, then thawed and frosted or decorated. Freeze in resealable plastic freezer bags, marking them clearly with the date. Keep frozen for up to 3 months. Let thaw completely at room temperature.

CHAPTER ONE

. . . .

Fruit Muffins

Raisin Bran Muffins

These are classic raisin bran muffins. The batter can be prepared ahead and kept in the refrigerator for up to two weeks, allowing you to bake a few muffins fresh each day for breakfast or for your lunchbox. The recipe is also easily halved.

Makes 36

1 cup/225 ml boiling water
5 tsp baking soda
1 cup/225 g vegetable shortening
2 cups/450 g sugar
2 eggs, lightly beaten
2 tbsp molasses
5 cups/750 g all-purpose flour
4½ cups/300 g All-Bran cereal
2 cups/100 g bran flakes
2 cups/300 g raisins
1 tbsp salt
4 cups/900 ml buttermilk

1. Preheat the oven to 400°F/200°C. Grease however many muffin cups you wish to use (up to 36) or line a pan with muffin cups.

2. In a very large bowl, pour the boiling water over the baking soda. Stir until dissolved, then let cool. In another bowl, cream the shortening and sugar until light and fluffy, then gradually beat in the eggs. Stir in the molasses.

3. In another bowl, mix together the flour, All-Bran, bran flakes, raisins, and salt.

4. Add the buttermilk to the baking soda mixture. Add about half the wet and dry ingredients alternately to the creamed mixture. Blend in the remaining wet and dry ingredients, stirring until just combined.

5. Spoon the batter evenly into the prepared pan and bake until risen and firm, about 20 minutes. Cool in the pan for 10 minutes, then turn out onto a wire rack. Serve warm or cold, spread with a little butter.

Date Bran Muffins

Make the batter for these muffins the day before you want to bake them, as the batter needs to rest overnight.

Makes 12

2 cups/300 g all-purpose flour
1 tsp baking soda
1 tsp ground cinnamon
½ cup/125 g sugar
Generous 1½ cups/80 g wheat bran
¾ cup/120 g pitted dates, finely chopped
½ cup/125 ml buttermilk
¾ cup/175 ml milk
¼ cup/50 ml vegetable oil
1 egg, lightly beaten

1. Mix the flour, baking soda, cinnamon, and sugar in a large bowl. Add the bran and dates and mix well. Mix the buttermilk, milk, oil, and egg together in a small bowl, then add to the dry ingredients. Mix briefly, then cover and refrigerate overnight.

2. Next day, preheat the oven to 400°F/200°C. Grease a 12-cup muffin pan or line with muffin cups.

3. Spoon the batter evenly into the prepared pan and bake until risen and golden, about 20 minutes. Cool in the pan for 10 minutes, then turn out onto a wire rack. Serve warm or cold.

Rhubarb Almond Muffins

Rhubarb and almonds are a classic combination. These muffins would also be very tasty with chopped fresh strawberries replacing the prunes.

Makes 12

⅔ lb/275 g rhubarb, tops removed and
    ends trimmed
2 cups/300 g all-purpose flour
⅓ cup/50 g blanched almonds, chopped
1 tbsp baking powder
1 tsp baking soda
½ tsp grated nutmeg
½ tsp salt
¼ tsp ground cinnamon
1 cup/200 g packed light brown sugar
1¼ cups/300 ml buttermilk
½ cup/125 ml vegetable oil
1 egg, lightly beaten
1 tbsp vanilla extract
Generous ½ cup/100 g prunes, pitted
    and chopped

1. Preheat the oven to 375°F/190°C. Grease a 12-cup muffin pan or line with muffin cups.

2. Wash the rhubarb stalks, chop coarsely, and set aside. In a large bowl, mix the flour, almonds, baking powder, baking soda, nutmeg, salt, and cinnamon.

3. In another bowl, beat the brown sugar, buttermilk, oil, egg, and vanilla. Stir into the flour mixture until just combined. Fold in the rhubarb and prunes.

4. Spoon the batter evenly into the prepared pan. Bake until risen and golden, 18 to 20 minutes. Let cool in the pan for 5 minutes, then turn out onto a wire rack. Serve warm or cold.

Apple, Cheese, and Oat Muffins

This unusual combination is positively delicious. Try serving these tasty and wholesome muffins for breakfast.

Makes 12

1⅓ cups/225 g oat bran
½ cup/75 g wholewheat flour
¼ cup/50 g packed brown sugar
1½ tbsp baking powder
1 tsp ground cinnamon
½ tsp salt
½ cup/125 ml apple juice
¼ cup/50 ml skim milk
1 egg, lightly beaten
2 tbsp light vegetable oil
2 tbsp honey
1 medium apple, peeled and diced
⅔ cup/75 g cheddar cheese, cut into
    small cubes
3 tbsp rolled oats

1. Preheat the oven to 400°F/200°C. Grease a 12-cup muffin pan or line with muffin cups.

2. Combine the oat bran, flour, brown sugar, baking powder, cinnamon, and salt in a large bowl. In another bowl, mix the apple juice, milk, egg, oil, and honey. Add the wet ingredients to the dry ingredients along with the diced apple and cheese and mix until just combined.

3. Spoon the batter evenly into the prepared pan, sprinkle over rolled oats, and bake until risen and golden, about 20 minutes. Cool in the pan for 10 minutes, then turn out onto a wire rack. Serve warm or cold.

Wholewheat Banana Walnut Muffins

The wholewheat flour in this recipe really emphasizes the nutty flavor.

Makes 12

1 cup/150 g self-rising wholewheat flour
1 cup/150 g self-rising flour
2 tbsp packed brown sugar
½ cup/65 g chopped walnuts
3 large very ripe bananas, peeled
¼ cup/50 ml vegetable oil
2 eggs, lightly beaten
⅓ cup/80 ml sour cream
2 tbsp honey

1. Preheat the oven to 400°F/200°C. Grease a 12-cup muffin pan or line with muffin cups.

2. Mix the flours in a large bowl. Add the brown sugar and walnuts and mix well. In another bowl, mash the bananas until fairly smooth, then stir in the oil, eggs, sour cream, and honey. Add the wet ingredients to the dry ingredients all at once and mix briefly until just combined. Spoon the batter evenly into the prepared pan and bake until risen and golden, about 20 minutes.

3. Cool in the pan for 10 minutes, then turn out onto a wire rack. Serve warm or cold.

Pear and Walnut Muffins with Butterscotch Sauce

Makes 12

2 cups/300 g all-purpose flour
2 tsp baking powder
½ tsp baking soda
1 cup/225 g sugar
¼ tsp salt
1 tsp ground cinnamon
1 tsp ground cardamom
2 eggs, lightly beaten
¾ cup/175 ml sour cream
¾ cup/1½ sticks/175 g butter, melted
3 canned pear halves, drained and diced
½ cup/65 g coarsely chopped walnuts

For the butterscotch sauce:
1 cup/200 g packed dark brown sugar
½ cup/1 stick/125 g butter
4 tbsp whipping cream

1. Preheat the oven to 400°F/200°C.
Grease a 12-cup muffin pan or line with
muffin cups.

2. In a large bowl, mix the flour, baking
powder, baking soda, sugar, salt, cinnamon,
and cardamom.

3. In another bowl, whisk together the
eggs, sour cream, and melted butter. Add
the wet ingredients to the dry ingredients
along with the pear and walnuts and mix
briefly until just combined.

4. Spoon the batter evenly into the
prepared pan. Bake until risen and golden,
20 to 25 minutes.

5. Meanwhile, for the sauce combine the
brown sugar and butter in a pan and place
over very low heat until the butter has
melted and the sugar has dissolved; do not
boil. Remove from heat and add the
whipping cream. Mix well and keep warm.

6. When the muffins are baked, cool in the
pan for 10 minutes, then serve warm
drizzled with the sauce.

Granola-topped Applesauce Muffins

Using ready-made applesauce and granola makes these muffins a cinch. Use a granola with raisins and nuts for added crunch and sweetness.

Makes 12

2 cups/300 g all-purpose flour
½ cup/100 g packed light brown sugar
1 tbsp baking powder
½ tsp baking soda
½ tsp salt
½ tsp ground cinnamon
½ tsp grated nutmeg
4 tbsp butter, melted
1⅓ cups/300 g applesauce
¼ cup/50 ml milk
1 egg, lightly beaten
½ cup/75 g granola

1. Preheat the oven to 425°F/220°C. Grease a 12-cup muffin pan, or line with muffin cups.

2. In a large bowl, mix the flour, brown sugar, baking powder, baking soda, salt, cinnamon, and nutmeg. In another bowl, mix the butter, applesauce, milk, and egg. Add the wet ingredients to the dry ingredients and stir briefly until just combined. Spoon the batter evenly into the prepared pan.

3. Place the granola into a bowl and crush lightly, using the back of a spoon or the end of a rolling pin, until the pieces are small and even. Sprinkle evenly over the muffin batter.

4. Bake the muffins until risen and golden, about 15 to 20 minutes. Cool in the pan for 10 minutes, then turn out onto a wire rack. Serve warm or cold.

Raspberry Cheesecake Muffins

*If you prefer, replace the raspberries
with other fresh berries such as
strawberries or blueberries.*

Makes 12

For the cheesecake mixture:
⅔ cup/150 g cream cheese, softened
¾ cup/160 g sugar
1 egg
½ tsp vanilla extract

For the muffin batter:
1 cup/225 ml milk
6 tbsp butter
1 tsp vanilla extract
2 eggs, lightly beaten
1½ cups/225 g all-purpose flour
½ cup/125 g sugar
2 tsp baking powder
½ tsp salt
⅔ cup/100 g fresh or frozen raspberries

1. Preheat the oven to 400°F/200°C. Grease a
12-cup muffin pan or line with muffin cups.

2. For the cheesecake mixture, combine the
cream cheese, sugar, egg, and vanilla in a
bowl, mixing well. Set aside.

3. For the batter, combine the milk, butter,
and vanilla in a pan and stir over low heat
until the butter is melted. Remove from the
heat and let cool. Beat in the eggs.

4. In a large bowl, mix the flour, sugar,
baking powder, and salt. Add the milk
mixture and stir until just combined. Fold
in the raspberries.

5. Spoon the batter evenly into the prepared
pan. Top each muffin with 2 teaspoons of the
cream cheese mixture and swirl slightly with
a knife. Bake until the tops spring back when
lightly touched, about 20 minutes. Cool in
the pan for 10 minutes, then turn out onto a
wire rack. Serve warm or cold.

Cranberry and Pecan Muffins with Cinnamon

These muffins would also be very tasty with juicy raisins in place of the cranberries, if you prefer.

Makes 12

2 cups/300 g all-purpose flour
½ cup/100 g packed brown sugar
¼ cup/50 g granulated sugar
2 tsp baking powder
1 tsp salt
1 tsp ground cinnamon
Scant 1¼ cups/275 ml milk
½ cup/125 ml vegetable oil
1 egg, lightly beaten
1 cup/150 g dried cranberries
⅓ cup/50 g chopped pecans

1. Preheat the oven to 350°F/180°C. Grease a 12-cup muffin pan or line with muffin cups.

2. Combine flour, sugars, baking powder, salt, and cinnamon in a medium bowl. In another bowl, combine the milk, oil, and egg.

3. Add the wet ingredients to the dry ingredients, stirring until just combined. Stir in the cranberries and nuts.

4. Spoon the batter evenly into the prepared pan and bake until risen and golden, about 25 minutes. Cool for 5 minutes in the pan, then turn out onto a wire rack to cool for 10 minutes. Serve warm or cold.

Apricot Muffins with Vanilla and Lemon

*These are classy muffins, with a
beautiful fresh vanilla fragrance. If
you don't have a vanilla bean, add
1 teaspoon of good-quality vanilla
extract to the wet ingredients and
add the sugar to the dry ingredients.*

Makes 12

½ vanilla bean
1 cup/225 g sugar
2 cups/300 g all-purpose flour
1 tbsp baking powder
¾ tsp salt
½ cup/1 stick/125 g butter
½ cup/100 g chopped, ready-to-eat,
  dried apricots
Finely grated peel of 1 lemon
1 egg, lightly beaten
1 cup/225 ml milk

1. Preheat the oven to 400°F/200°C.
Grease a 12-cup muffin pan or line with
muffin cups.

2. Put the vanilla bean and sugar into a
blender or food processor and blend until
the vanilla bean is very finely chopped. In
a large bowl, mix together the flour, baking
powder, and salt. Stir in the vanilla sugar.

3. Using the tips of your fingers, rub in the
butter until the mixture resembles fine
breadcrumbs. Stir in the dried apricots
and lemon peel.

4. Combine the egg and milk and add to
flour mixture. Stir the mixture briefly until
just combined.

5. Spoon the batter evenly into the
prepared pan and bake until risen and
golden, 20 to 25 minutes. Cool in the pan
for 10 minutes, then turn out onto a wire
rack. Serve warm or cold.

Cranberry Orange Muffins

This classic combination is enhanced with chopped pecans to give a satisfying crunch and texture.

Makes 12

2 cups/300 g all-purpose flour
1 cup/225 g sugar
1 tbsp baking powder
½ tsp salt
¾ cup/125 g fresh or frozen cranberries (thawed if frozen), coarsely chopped
Finely grated peel of 1 orange
2 tbsp chopped pecans
1 egg, lightly beaten
1 cup/225 ml milk
3 tbsp melted butter

1. Preheat the oven to 450°F/230°C. Grease a 12-cup muffin pan or line with muffin cups.

2. Mix the flour, sugar, baking powder, and salt into a large bowl. Stir in the cranberries, orange peel, and pecans.

3. In another bowl, mix the egg, milk, and butter. Add to the dry ingredients and stir until just combined.

4. Spoon the batter evenly into the prepared pan and bake until risen and golden, 18 to 20 minutes. Cool in the pan for 10 minutes, then turn out onto a wire rack. Serve warm or cold.

Peach and Basil Muffins

Use only the freshest peaches in season to get the best result. If you want to make these muffins out of season, use well-drained, canned peaches packed in juice.

Makes 12

2 ripe peaches, peeled and pitted
2 tbsp chopped fresh basil
3 tbsp packed brown sugar
Grated peel and juice of ½ lemon
2 cups/300 g self-rising flour
½ tsp baking powder
4 tbsp butter
Generous ⅓ cup/80 g granulated sugar
1 egg, lightly beaten
⅔ cup/150 ml milk

1. Chop the peaches into small dice, then place in a bowl with the basil, brown sugar, and lemon juice. Let stand for about 30 minutes.

2. Preheat the oven to 400°F/200°C. Grease a 12-cup muffin pan or line with muffin cups.

3. In a large bowl, mix the flour and baking powder. Rub in the butter until the mixture resembles fine breadcrumbs. Stir in the granulated sugar and lemon peel.

4. In another bowl, mix the egg and milk. Add this to the dry mixture alternately with the peaches and their juices.

5. Spoon the mixture into the prepared pan and bake until risen and golden, about 20 minutes. Cool in the pan for 10 minutes, then turn out onto a wire rack. Serve warm or cold.

Cherry Coconut Muffins

Don't try using fresh cherries in this one—they add too much moisture to the batter. These muffins are best made in a nonstick muffin pan, rather than with paper liners.

Makes 12

2 cups/300 g self-rising flour
4 tbsp soft margarine
⅔ cup/150 g chopped, candied cherries
1 cup/100 g flaked coconut
1 tbsp sugar
¼ tsp salt
2 eggs, lightly beaten
1 cup/225 ml milk

1. Preheat the oven to 400°F/200°C. Grease a 12-cup nonstick muffin pan.

2. Put the flour in a bowl with the margarine and blend with a fork until evenly mixed. Stir in the cherries, coconut, sugar, and salt until well mixed.

3. In another bowl, beat the eggs and milk until well combined, then add to the dry ingredients. Stir until just mixed.

4. Spoon the batter into the prepared pan and bake until risen and golden, 15 to 20 minutes. Cool in the pan for 10 minutes, then turn out onto a wire rack. Serve warm or cold.

Blueberry Muffins

Someone once said that "When a man grows tired of blueberry muffins, he grows tired of life."

Makes 12

2 cups/300 g self-rising flour
1 tsp baking powder
4 tbsp butter
Generous ⅓ cup/80 g sugar
1 cup/150 g fresh blueberries
2 eggs, lightly beaten
1 cup/225 ml milk
1 tsp vanilla extract

1. Preheat the oven to 400°F/200°C. Grease a 12-cup muffin pan or line with muffin cups.

2. Mix the flour and baking powder in a large bowl. Rub in the butter until the mixture resembles fine breadcrumbs. Stir in the sugar and blueberries.

3. In another small bowl, thoroughly beat together the eggs, milk, and vanilla. Pour the mixture all at once into the dry ingredients. Mix until just combined.

4. Spoon the batter evenly into the prepared pan and bake until risen and golden, about 25 minutes. Cool in the pan for 10 minutes, then turn out onto a wire rack. Serve warm or cold.

Plum and Marzipan Muffins

The marzipan softens and melts a little during the baking of these muffins and tastes fabulous with the tart, fresh plums.

Makes 12

1 cup/150 g all-purpose flour
1 cup/150 g wholewheat flour
1 cup/100 g rolled oats
4 tsp baking powder
¾ tsp salt
1 cup/50 g wheat bran
¾ cup/150 g packed brown sugar
1½ cups/250 g chopped unpeeled plums
¾ cup/175 ml orange juice
½ cup/125 ml vegetable oil
2 eggs, lightly beaten
Finely grated peel of ½ orange
½ cup/100 g marzipan, cut into small
   cubes
¼ cup/25 g sliced almonds

1. Preheat the oven to 350°F/180°C. Grease a 12-cup muffin pan or line with muffin cups.

2. In a large bowl, mix the flours, oats, baking powder, salt, bran, and brown sugar. In another bowl, mix the plums, orange juice, oil, eggs, and orange peel.

3. Add the wet ingredients to the dry ingredients along with the marzipan and almonds and stir until just combined.

4. Spoon the batter evenly into the prepared pan and bake until risen and golden, about 30 minutes. Cool in the pan for 10 minutes, then turn out onto a wire rack. Serve warm or cold.

Clementine Muffins

If fresh clementines are unavailable, substitute a small can of mandarin segments, well drained and chopped.

Makes 12

2 cups/300 g all-purpose flour
2 tsp baking powder
½ tsp salt
¼ tsp ground allspice
¼ tsp grated nutmeg
Generous ½ cup/125 g sugar
⅓ cup/60 g margarine or butter
1 egg, lightly beaten
⅞ cup/200 ml milk
3 clementines or mandarin oranges, peeled, sectioned, and chopped

For the topping (optional):
Generous ¼ cup/65 g sugar
½ tsp ground cinnamon
4 tbsp butter, melted

1. Preheat the oven to 350°F/180°C. Grease a 12-cup muffin pan or line with muffin cups.

2. Mix the flour with the baking powder, salt, spices, and sugar in a large bowl. Rub in the margarine or butter.

3. In another bowl, mix the egg and milk, and add all at once to the dry ingredients. Mix briefly until just combined. Fold in the clementine pieces.

4. Spoon the batter evenly into the prepared pan and bake until risen and golden, 20 to 25 minutes. Meanwhile, for the topping, mix the sugar and cinnamon and set aside. Remove the muffins from the pan while still warm. Dip the tops in melted butter, then in the cinnamon sugar. Let cool for 10 minutes.

Sour Cherry Muffins Filled with Jam

If you don't have any fresh cherries, use canned or bottled pitted cherries. Make sure they are well drained.

Makes 12

2 cups/300 g all-purpose flour
1 tsp baking powder
½ tsp baking soda
½ tsp salt
½ tsp ground cardamom
Generous ½ cup/125 g sugar
1 cup/150 g fresh cherries, pitted and
    coarsely chopped
4 tbsp butter, melted
1 egg, lightly beaten
1 cup/225 ml sour cream
½ tsp vanilla extract
3 tbsp sour cherry jam
3 tbsp slivered almonds

1. Preheat the oven to 400°F/200°C. Grease a 12-cup muffin pan or line with muffin cups.

2. Mix the flour, baking powder, baking soda, salt, and cardamom in a large bowl. Stir in the sugar and cherries and mix well.

3. In another bowl, beat the butter, egg, sour cream, and vanilla together. Pour the wet ingredients into the flour mixture and fold together until just blended.

4. Spoon half the batter evenly into the prepared pan cups. Add about 1 teaspoon of sour cherry jam to each, then top with the remaining batter. Sprinkle with the slivered almonds. Bake until risen and golden, about 20 minutes.

5. Cool in the pan for 10 minutes, then turn out onto a wire rack. Serve warm or cold.

Spiced Caramel Orange Muffins

This recipe is a little more trouble than some, but produces a fabulous result. Try the muffins at Christmas, when the smell of them baking will scent your whole house.

Makes 12

1 large orange
Generous ½ cup/125 g sugar
2 tbsp water
2¼ cups/340 g self-rising flour
1 tsp baking powder
½ tsp ground cinnamon
¼ tsp ground cloves
¼ tsp ground allspice
Pinch of salt
4 tbsp butter
⅓ cup/80 g sugar
½ cup/65 g chopped pistachios
2 eggs, lightly beaten
1 cup/225 ml milk

1. Preheat the oven to 400°F/200°C. Grease a 12-cup muffin pan or line with muffin cups.

2. To make the caramel oranges, remove the peel and pith of the orange by cutting it away in strips using a small, sharp knife. Working over a bowl to collect any juice, section the orange by cutting carefully between the membranes separating the segments. Coarsely chop the orange sections and add to the bowl. Set aside.

3. Combine the sugar and water in a small pan and stir over low heat until the sugar has dissolved, making sure there are no sugar crystals clinging to the side of the pan. Wash the pan down using a pastry brush dipped in water, if necessary. Raise the heat and bring to a boil. Boil for about 7 to 10 minutes or until the sugar has turned a dark caramel color. (Let the caramel darken as far as you dare without burning.) Remove the pan from the heat and, being careful to avoid splashes, add the orange and all its juice. Be careful: the mixture will bubble fiercely but just stand back. Let cool, then drain the oranges, reserving ¾ cup/175 ml of the syrup.

4. Mix the flour, baking powder, spices, and salt in a large bowl. Rub in the butter until the mixture resembles fine breadcrumbs, then thoroughly stir in the sugar and pistachios.

5. In another small bowl, whisk together the eggs and milk, then pour the mixture all at once into the dry ingredients. Add the drained oranges and mix briefly until just combined. Spoon the batter evenly into the prepared pan.

6. Bake until well risen, golden, and firm to the touch, 18 to 20 minutes. Remove from the oven and spoon the reserved orange syrup over the hot muffins. Let the muffins cool in the pan for 10 minutes. Serve warm or cold.

Tropical Fruit Muffins with Passion Fruit Glaze

Note: these muffins are not suitable for freezing.

Makes 12

1 very ripe, small mango
2 cups/300 g all-purpose flour
4 tsp baking powder
½ tsp salt
1 cup/225 g sugar
½ cup/50 g flaked coconut
¼ cup/50 ml vegetable oil
1 cup/225 ml milk
1 egg, lightly beaten
1 cup/215 g canned crushed
    pineapple in juice, drained
4 ripe passion fruit
4 tbsp sugar

1. Preheat the oven to 400°F/200°C. Grease a 12-cup muffin pan or line with muffin cups.

2. Peel the mango and cut the flesh away from the seed. Puree the flesh in a food processor. Set aside.

3. Mix the flour, baking powder, salt, and sugar in a large bowl. Stir in the coconut. In another bowl, combine the oil, milk, and egg. Add the wet ingredients to the dry ingredients and mix until just combined. Fold in the mango and drained pineapple.

4. Spoon the batter evenly into the prepared pan. Bake until risen and golden, 15 to 18 minutes.

5. Meanwhile, scoop the pulp and seeds from the passion fruit and press through a strainer into a small pan. Add the sugar and stir over low heat until dissolved. Raise the heat and bring to a boil. Cook for 3 minutes or until syrupy. Remove from the heat.

6. Remove the muffins from the oven and spoon the passion fruit syrup over while still hot. Let cool in the pan. Serve warm or just cooled.

Carrot, Apple, and Coconut Muffins

An unusual combination that makes very moist muffins. Dried apple is readily available from health food stores and many large supermakets.

Makes 12

1 cup/150 g wholewheat flour
1 cup/150 g all-purpose flour
¾ cup/175 g sugar
2 tsp baking powder
1 tsp ground cinnamon
½ tsp baking soda
1 cup/200 g finely grated carrot
Scant 1 cup/100 g dried apple, chopped
½ cup/75 g raisins
⅓ cup/50 g chopped walnuts
½ cup/50 g flaked coconut
2 eggs, lightly beaten
½ cup/125 ml buttermilk
½ cup/125 ml milk
2 tsp vanilla extract

1. Preheat the oven to 350°F/180°C. Grease a 12-cup muffin pan or line with muffin cups.

2. In a large bowl, stir together the flours, sugar, baking powder, cinnamon, and baking soda. Stir in the carrot, apple, raisins, walnuts, and coconut.

3. In another bowl, stir together the eggs, buttermilk, milk, and vanilla. Add the wet ingredients to the dry ingredients all at once and stir briefly until just combined. Carefully spoon the batter evenly into the prepared pan.

4. Bake until risen and golden, 20 to 25 minutes. Cool in the pan for 10 minutes, then turn out onto a wire rack. Serve warm or cold.

Date, Banana, and Hazelnut Muffins

To toast hazelnuts, or any other nuts for that matter, put them in a single layer on a baking sheet and put into a hot oven for about 5 minutes (smaller nuts may take less time while larger nuts may need a couple of minutes more) until golden and fragrant.

Makes 12

2 cups/300 g self-rising flour
2 tbsp packed brown sugar
⅓ cup/50 g chopped, toasted hazelnuts
3 large very ripe bananas, peeled
¼ cup/50 ml vegetable oil
2 eggs, lightly beaten
⅓ cup/80 ml plain yogurt
2 tbsp demerara sugar

1. Preheat the oven to 400°F/200°C. Grease a 12-cup muffin pan or line with muffin cups.

2. In a large bowl mix together the flour, brown sugar, and hazelnuts.

3. In another bowl, mash the bananas until fairly smooth, then stir in the oil, eggs, and yogurt. Add the wet ingredients to the dry ingredients all at once, and mix briefly until just combined.

4. Spoon the batter evenly into the prepared pan and sprinkle with the demerara sugar. Bake until risen and golden, about 20 minutes. Cool in the pan for 10 minutes, then turn out onto a wire rack. Serve warm or cold.

Cottage Cheese and Raisin Muffins

An unusual combination of savory and sweet that works really well and makes very moist muffins.

Makes 12

2 cups/300 g all-purpose flour
1½ cups/375 g All-Bran cereal
¾ cup/175 g sugar
1 tbsp baking powder
½ tsp baking soda
1 tsp ground cinnamon
1 tsp finely grated orange peel
½ tsp salt
Generous 1 cup/250 g cottage cheese
1 cup/225 ml plain yogurt
2 tbsp honey
4 tbsp butter, melted
2 eggs, lightly beaten
½ cup/100 g grated carrots
½ cup/75 g raisins

For the topping:
2 tbsp sugar
1 tsp ground cinnamon

1. Preheat the oven to 400°F/200°C. Grease a 12-cup muffin pan or line with muffin cups.

2. In a large bowl, combine the flour, All-Bran, sugar, baking powder, baking soda, cinnamon, orange peel, and salt.

3. In another bowl, mix the cottage cheese, yogurt, honey, melted butter, and eggs. Add the wet ingredients to the dry ingredients and mix until just combined. Fold in the carrots and raisins.

4. Spoon the batter evenly into the prepared pan. Combine the sugar and cinnamon for the topping and sprinkle over the muffins. Bake until risen and golden, about 25 minutes. Cool in the pan for 10 minutes, then turn out onto a wire rack. Serve warm or cold.

Pineapple Coconut Muffins

Like a pina colada without the rum, these muffins owe their moist texture to the combination of rich pineapple and coconut—a little taste of the tropics in one bite!

Makes 12

2 cups/300 g all-purpose flour
4 tsp baking powder
½ teaspoon salt
1 cup/225 g sugar
¾ cup/50 g freshly grated coconut
¼ cup/50 ml vegetable oil
1 cup/225 ml milk
1 egg, lightly beaten
⅔ cup/150 g canned crushed
    pineapple in juice, drained

1. Preheat the oven to 400°F/200°C. Grease a 12-cup muffin pan or line with muffin cups.

2. Mix the flour, baking powder, salt, and sugar together in a large bowl. Stir in the fresh coconut.

3. In another bowl, combine the oil, milk, and egg. Add the wet ingredients to the dry ingredients and mix until just combined, then stir in the drained pineapple.

4. Spoon the batter evenly into the prepared muffin pan. Bake until risen and golden, 15 to 18 minutes. Cool in the pan for 10 minutes, then turn out onto a wire rack. Serve warm or cold.

Honey Oat Bran Muffins

Oat bran should be easy to find in food stores alongside the Scotch oats, but if you have any trouble, try your local health food store.

Makes 12

1 cup/150 g self-rising wholewheat flour
1⅓ cups/200 g self-rising flour
½ tsp pumpkin pie spice
5 tbsp packed light brown sugar
1 tbsp baking powder
⅓ cup/60 g oat bran
⅔ cup/100 g golden raisins
6 tbsp vegetable oil
3 tbsp honey, plus about 3 tbsp to drizzle
2 eggs, lightly beaten
1 cup/225 ml milk

1. Preheat the oven to 400°F/200°C. Grease a 12-cup muffin pan or line with muffin cups.

2. Mix the flours, spice, brown sugar, baking powder, and oat bran in a large bowl. Add the golden raisins and mix well.

3. In another bowl, mix the oil, honey, eggs, and milk. Add this to the dry ingredients and mix until just combined.

4. Spoon the batter evenly into the prepared pan and bake until risen and golden, 20 to 25 minutes. Drizzle about 1 teaspoon honey over each of the hot muffins. Cool in the pan for 10 minutes, then turn out onto a wire rack. Serve warm or cold.

Lime and Fresh Coconut Muffins

Fresh coconuts are not difficult to deal with, but you must drain the juice out before cracking them open completely. Using a metal skewer, punch a hole in two of the three "eyes" at one end of the coconut and drain the juice. Bash the coconut as hard as you can with a hammer to open, then extract the flesh before grating.

Makes 12

1½ cups/100 g freshly grated coconut
2 cups/300 g self-rising flour
1 cup/225 g sugar
Grated peel and juice of 3 limes
1 egg, lightly beaten
1 cup/225 ml milk
⅓ cup/60 g butter, melted

1. Preheat the oven to 400°F/200°C. Grease a 12-cup muffin pan or line with muffin cups.

2. Set aside about 3 tablespoons of the grated coconut. In a large bowl, mix the flour and sugar. Add the remaining coconut and the lime peel. Mix well.

3. In another bowl, mix the lime juice, egg, milk, and butter. Add to the dry ingredients and stir until just mixed.

4. Spoon the batter evenly into the prepared pan and sprinkle with the reserved coconut. Bake until risen and golden, about 20 minutes. Cool in the pan for 10 minutes, then turn onto a wire rack. Serve warm or cold.

Dried Cherry, Apple, and Pecan Muffins

If dried cherries are unavailable, try making these delicious muffins with dried cranberries.

Makes 12

2 cups/300 g all-purpose flour
1 cup/225 g sugar
1 tbsp baking powder
½ tsp salt
1 large apple, coarsely chopped
  with skin
1 cup/150 g dried cherries, coarsely
  chopped
⅔ cup/75 g pecans, chopped
2 eggs, lightly beaten
½ cup/1 stick/125 g butter, melted
¾ cup/175 ml buttermilk
3 tbsp demerara sugar
1 tsp ground cinnamon

1. Preheat the oven to 400°F/200°C. Grease a 12-cup muffin pan or line with muffin cups.

2. In a large bowl, mix the flour, sugar, baking powder, and salt. Stir in the apple, cherries, and pecans.

3. In another bowl, mix the eggs, butter, and buttermilk. Add to the dry ingredients all at once and mix briefly until just combined.

4. Spoon the batter into the prepared pan. Mix the demerara sugar and cinnamon and sprinkle evenly over the muffins. Bake until risen and golden, 25 to 30 minutes. Cool in the pan for 10 minutes, then turn out onto a wire rack. Serve warm or cold.

Pumpkin, Maple Syrup, and Walnut Muffins

Makes 12

For the filling:
⅓ cup/75 g cream cheese, softened
2 tbsp packed brown sugar
2 tbsp maple syrup

For the muffin batter:
2 cups/300 g all-purpose flour
2 tsp baking powder
½ tsp baking soda
1 tsp ground cinnamon
½ tsp grated nutmeg
¼ tsp salt
¾ cup/150 g packed brown sugar
½ cup/65 g chopped walnuts
2 eggs, lightly beaten
Generous 1 cup/250 g pumpkin puree,
   fresh or canned
¾ cup/175 ml evaporated milk
¼ cup/50 ml vegetable oil
1 tbsp maple syrup

For the topping:
1 tbsp packed brown sugar
¼ cup/30 g chopped walnuts

1. Preheat the oven to 400°F/200°C. Grease a 12-cup muffin pan or line with muffin cups.

2. For the filling, blend the cream cheese, brown sugar, and maple syrup until smooth.

3. For the muffin batter, mix the flour, baking powder, baking soda, cinnamon, nutmeg, and salt in a bowl. Stir in the sugar and nuts. In another bowl, mix the eggs, pumpkin, evaporated milk, oil, and maple syrup.

4. Add the wet ingredients to the dry ingredients all at once and mix briefly until just combined. Fold in the filling mixture until the batter is just swirled through.

5. For the topping, mix the brown sugar and nuts in a small bowl.

6. Spoon the batter into the prepared pan and sprinkle with the topping mixture. Bake until risen and golden, 20 to 25 minutes. Cool in the pan for 10 minutes, then turn out onto a wire rack. Serve warm or cold.

Spiced Carrot Muffins with Cream Cheese Topping

These muffins are really mini carrot cakes. Perfect for lunchboxes and afternoon tea.

Makes 12

2 cups/300 g all-purpose flour
1 cup/225 g sugar
2 tsp baking soda
2 tsp ground cinnamon
1 tsp salt
¾ cup/175 ml vegetable oil
¾ cup/175 ml milk
3 eggs, lightly beaten
½ cup/100 g grated carrot
1 cup/120 g chopped walnuts
1 cup/150 g raisins

For the topping:
Generous ⅓ cup/85 g cream cheese, softened
3 tbsp butter, softened
1 cup/125 g confectioners' sugar
½ tsp vanilla extract

1. Preheat the oven to 350°F/180°C. Grease a 12-cup muffin pan or line with muffin cups.

2. Mix the flour, sugar, baking soda, cinnamon, and salt into a large bowl. In another bowl, whisk together the oil, milk, and eggs. Add the wet ingredients to the dry ingredients all at once along with the carrot, walnuts, and raisins. Mix briefly until just combined.

3. Spoon the batter evenly into the prepared pan and bake until risen and golden, 20 to 25 minutes. Turn out onto a wire rack and let cool completely, for 10 minutes.

4. Meanwhile, for the topping, beat the cream cheese and butter in a medium bowl until light and fluffy. Beat in the confectioners' sugar and vanilla until the topping is thick and spreadable. Spread a large tablespoonful on each muffin.

Lemon Poppy Seed Muffins

It's best to make these muffins in a nonstick muffin pan without paper liners so that the syrup can soak into the muffins without running under the paper.

Makes 12

Finely grated peel and juice of 2 lemons
1 cup/225 g sugar
2 cups/300 g self-rising flour
2 tbsp poppy seeds
1 egg, lightly beaten
1 cup/225 ml milk
⅓ cup/60 g butter, melted

For the lemon syrup:
¾ cup/100 g confectioners' sugar, sifted
Juice of 1 lemon

1. Preheat the oven to 400°F/200°C. Grease a 12-cup, preferably nonstick muffin pan.

2. Mix 2 teaspoons of the lemon peel and 2 tablespoons of the sugar. Set aside.

3. In a large bowl, mix the flour, poppy seeds, and remaining sugar. Add the remaining lemon peel with the lemon juice, egg, milk, and butter and stir until just combined.

4. Spoon the batter evenly into the prepared pan and sprinkle with the reserved sugar and lemon peel mixture. Bake until risen and golden, about 20 minutes.

5. Meanwhile, mix the confectioners' sugar and lemon juice until well blended. Spoon over the hot muffins and let cool in the pan. Serve cold.

Pear and Ginger Muffins

Leave the pears and pecans out of the batter for classic gingerbread muffins.

Makes 12

Generous 1 cup/125 g vegetable
    shortening, softened
Generous ½ cup/125 g sugar
Scant ¼ cup/50 g molasses
2 eggs, lightly beaten
1 tsp baking soda
¾ cup/175 ml buttermilk
2 cups/300 g all-purpose flour
½ tsp ground cinnamon
2 tsp ground ginger
⅛ tsp ground cloves
½ cup/65 g pecans, chopped
2 ripe pears, peeled and finely chopped

1. Preheat the oven to 350°F/180°C. Grease a 12-cup muffin pan or line with muffin cups.

2. In a mixing bowl, cream the shortening and sugar until light and fluffy. Stir in the molasses. Add the eggs one at a time, beating well after each addition.

3. Gently stir the baking soda into the buttermilk until it has dissolved.

4. In another bowl, mix the flour with the spices; add to the creamed mixture alternately with the buttermilk. Fold in the pecans and pears.

5. Spoon the batter evenly into the prepared pan and bake until risen and firm, about 20 minutes. Cool in the pan for 10 minutes, then turn out onto a wire rack. These muffins can be served warm or cold.

Peach Upside Down Muffins

Use chopped canned pineapple, if you prefer. These muffins are best made in a nonstick pan, rather than using paper liners.

Makes 12

⅓ cup/60 g cold butter, cut into 12 pieces
½ cup/100 g packed brown sugar
14 oz/400 g canned peach slices in juice, drained
1⅓ cups/200 g all-purpose flour
1 cup/225 g sugar
2 tsp baking powder
½ tsp salt
2 eggs, lightly beaten
⅔ cup/150 ml sour cream
2 tbsp/25 g vegetable shortening, melted

1. Preheat the oven to 375°F/190°C. Grease a 12-cup nonstick muffin pan.

2. Divide the butter and brown sugar evenly between the cups of the prepared pan. Place in the preheated oven until the butter and sugar have melted, about 5 minutes. Remove from the oven and arrange the peach slices in the bottoms of the muffin cups.

3. Meanwhile, in a large bowl, mix the flour, sugar, baking powder, and salt. In another bowl, mix the eggs, sour cream, and melted shortening. Add the wet ingredients to the dry ingredients all at once and mix briefly until just combined.

4. Spoon the batter evenly on top of the peach slices. Bake until risen and golden, about 25 minutes. Let cool in the pan for about 10 minutes, then invert onto a plate or platter. Serve warm.

CHAPTER TWO

· · · · · · · · · · ·

Chocolate Muffins

Vanilla Chocolate Chip Muffins

If you prefer, make mini muffins (this recipe makes 36). Freeze them to pop into lunchboxes, or keep them in an airtight container for quick pop-in-the-mouth snacks.

Makes 12

2 cups/300 g self-rising flour
1 tsp baking powder
4 tbsp butter
⅓ cup/80 g sugar
Scant 1 cup/150 g milk or semisweet
    chocolate chips
2 eggs, lightly beaten
1 cup/225 ml milk
1 tsp vanilla extract

1. Preheat the oven to 400°F/200°C. Grease a 12-cup muffin pan or line with muffin cups.

2. Mix the flour and baking powder in a large bowl. Rub in the butter until the mixture resembles fine breadcrumbs. Stir in the sugar and chocolate chips.

3. In a small bowl, whisk together the eggs, milk, and vanilla, then pour the mixture all at once into the dry ingredients. Mix quickly until just blended.

4. Spoon the batter evenly into the prepared pan and bake until well risen, golden, and firm to the touch, about 18 to 20 minutes. Cool in the pan for 10 minutes, then turn out onto a wire rack. Serve warm or cold.

White Chocolate Macadamia Nut Muffins

What a combination: moist chocolate muffins, studded with white chocolate and the king of nuts.

Makes 12

6 oz/175 g semisweet chocolate, coarsely
   chopped or broken
1½ cups/225 g all-purpose flour
¾ cup/150 g packed brown sugar
Generous ⅓ cup/35 g unsweetened
   cocoa powder
1 tsp baking powder
½ tsp salt
¾ cup/175 ml buttermilk
2 eggs, lightly beaten
1½ tsp vanilla extract
7 oz/200 g white chocolate, chopped
¾ cup/100 g unsalted macadamia nuts,
   coarsely chopped

1. Preheat the oven to 400°F/200°C.
Grease a 12-cup muffin pan or line with
muffin cups.

2. Put the semisweet chocolate into a
small heatproof bowl and set over a pan of
barely simmering water; do not allow the
bottom of the bowl to touch the water. Let
stand, stirring occasionally, until melted.
Stir until smooth. Set aside.

3. Mix the flour, brown sugar, cocoa,
baking powder, and salt in a large bowl. In
another bowl, mix the buttermilk, eggs,
and vanilla until blended.

4. Add the buttermilk mixture and
reserved chocolate mixture to the dry
ingredients and mix briefly until just
blended. Fold in the white chocolate and
macadamia nuts.

5. Spoon the batter evenly into the
prepared pan and bake until firm and well
risen, 25 to 30 minutes. Cool in the pan for
5 minutes, then turn out onto a wire rack.
Serve warm or cold.

White Chocolate, Lemon, and Raspberry Muffins

You can use frozen raspberries in this recipe if fresh are unavailable. You don't even need to thaw them first.

Makes 12

2 cups/300 g self-rising flour
1 tsp baking powder
4 tbsp butter
⅓ cup/80 g sugar
⅔ cup/100 g raspberries
5 oz/150 g white chocolate, coarsely
  chopped
Grated peel of 1 lemon
2 eggs, lightly beaten
1 cup/225 ml milk

1. Preheat the oven to 400°F/200°C. Grease a 12-cup muffin pan or line with muffin cups.

2. Mix the flour and baking powder in a large bowl. Rub in the butter until the mixture resembles fine breadcrumbs. Stir in the sugar, raspberries, white chocolate, and lemon peel.

3. In a small bowl, whisk together the eggs and milk, then pour the mixture all at once into the dry ingredients and mix briefly until just blended.

4. Spoon the batter evenly into the prepared pan and bake until well risen, golden, and firm to the touch, 18 to 20 minutes. Cool in the pan for 5 minutes, then turn out onto a wire rack. Serve warm or cold.

Double Chocolate Chip Muffins

For true chocolate lovers who just can't get enough.

Makes 12

2 cups/300 g all-purpose flour
1 cup/200 g packed brown sugar
Generous ⅓ cup/35 g unsweetened
   cocoa powder
2 tsp baking soda
½ tsp salt
1½ cups/350 ml milk
6 tbsp butter or margarine, melted
2 eggs, lightly beaten
Scant 1 cup/150 g semisweet
   chocolate chips

1. Preheat oven to 400°F/200°C. Grease a 12-cup muffin pan or line with muffin cups.

2. Mix together the flour, brown sugar, cocoa, baking soda, and salt in a large bowl. In another bowl, mix the milk, butter, and eggs. Add the wet ingredients to the dry ingredients all at once and mix briefly until just blended. Fold in the chocolate chips.

3. Spoon the batter evenly into the prepared pan and bake until well risen, 25 to 30 minutes. Let cool in the pan for 5 minutes, then turn out onto a wire rack. Serve warm or cold.

Hazelnut Chocolate Chunk Muffins

Use the best semisweet chocolate you can find for these muffins—the combination of rich chocolate and crunchy hazelnuts is sublime.

Makes 12

2 cups/300 g all-purpose flour
1 cup/200 g packed brown sugar
Generous ⅓ cup/35 g unsweetened
   cocoa powder
2 tsp baking soda
½ tsp salt
1½ cups/350 ml milk
6 tbsp butter or margarine, melted
2 eggs, lightly beaten
5 oz/150 g coarsely chopped
   semisweet chocolate
⅔ cup/100 g toasted hazelnuts,
   coarsely chopped

1. Preheat the oven to 400°F/200°C. Grease a 12-cup muffin pan or line with muffin cups.

2. Mix together the flour, sugar, cocoa, baking soda, and salt in a large bowl. In another bowl, mix the milk, butter, and eggs. Add the wet ingredients to the dry ingredients all at once and mix briefly until just combined. Fold in the chopped chocolate and hazelnuts.

3. Spoon the batter evenly into the prepared pan and bake until well risen and firm, 25 to 30 minutes. Cool in the pan for 5 minutes, then turn out onto a wire rack. Serve warm or cold.

Banana, Walnut, and Chocolate Chip Muffins

These are really lovely served warm, when the chocolate and banana have that soft, melt-in-the-mouth quality.

Makes 12

2 cups/300 g self-rising flour
2 tbsp packed brown sugar
½ cup/60 g chopped walnuts
Generous ½ cup/100 g semisweet
    chocolate chips
2 ripe bananas (about ½ lb/250 g),
    peeled
3 tbsp vegetable oil
2 eggs, lightly beaten
½ cup/125 ml sour cream

1. Preheat the oven to 400°F/200°C. Grease a 12-cup muffin pan or line with muffin cups.

2. Mix together the flour, brown sugar, walnuts, and chocolate chips in a large bowl. In another bowl, mash the bananas until fairly smooth, then stir in the vegetable oil, eggs, and sour cream. Add the wet ingredients to the dry ingredients all at once, and mix until just combined.

3. Spoon the batter evenly into the prepared pan and bake until risen and golden, about 20 minutes. Cool in the pan for 10 minutes, then turn out onto a wire rack. Serve warm or cold.

Chocolate Filled Muffins

Makes 12

For the filling:
1½ tbsp butter, softened
⅔ cup/75 g confectioners' sugar
1½ tsp milk
½ tsp vanilla extract
2 oz/50 g semisweet chocolate, melted

For the muffins:
2 cups/300 g self-rising flour
1 tsp baking powder
4 tbsp butter
Generous ⅓ cup/80 g sugar
2 eggs, lightly beaten
1 cup/225 ml milk
1 tsp vanilla extract
2 tbsp finely chopped hazelnuts
1 tbsp demerara sugar

1. Preheat the oven to 400°F/200°C. Grease a 12-cup muffin pan or line with muffin cups.

2. For the filling, cream the butter in a small bowl. Gradually add the confectioners' sugar, beating until well blended. Beat in the milk, vanilla, and melted chocolate. Set aside.

3. For the muffins, mix the flour and baking powder in a large bowl. Rub in the butter until the mixture resembles fine breadcrumbs. Stir in the sugar. In a small bowl, whisk together the eggs, milk, and vanilla, then pour the mixture all at once into the dry ingredients and mix briefly until just blended.

4. Put a spoonful of the batter into each cup of the prepared pan. Drop a large teaspoonful of the filling on top, then cover with the remaining muffin batter.

5. Mix the chopped hazelnuts and demerara sugar and sprinkle this mixture evenly over the muffins.

6. Bake until well risen, golden, and firm to the touch, 18 to 20 minutes. Cool in the pan for 5 minutes, then turn out onto a wire rack. These are best served warm.

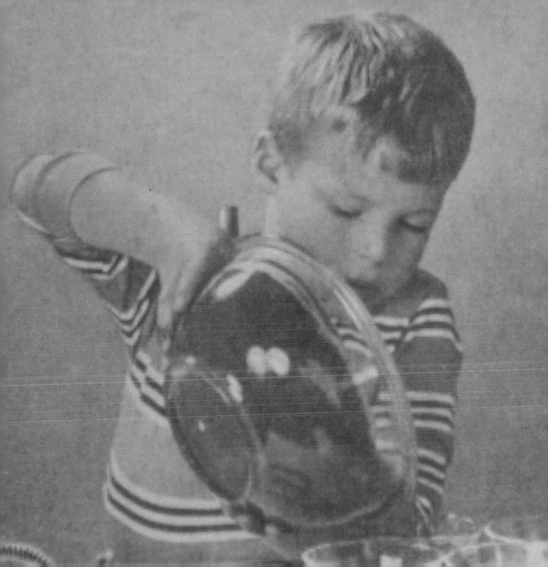

Chocolate Cheesecake Muffins

Makes 12

For the cheesecake mixture:
Generous ¾ cup/175 g cream cheese,
    room temperature
Generous ¼ cup/60 g sugar
1 egg, lightly beaten
⅛ tsp vanilla extract
¼ cup/25 g sliced almonds

For the muffins:
1 cup/150 g all-purpose flour
Generous ¾ cup/175 g sugar
Generous ⅓ cup/35 g unsweetened
    cocoa powder
½ tsp baking soda
¼ tsp salt
½ cup/125 ml sour cream
¼ cup/50 ml vegetable oil
4 tbsp butter, melted and cooled
2 eggs, lightly beaten
1 tsp vanilla extract
3 oz/75 g semisweet chocolate, melted

1. Preheat the oven to 375°F/190°C. Grease a 12-cup muffin pan or line with muffin cups.

2. For the cheesecake mixture, combine the cream cheese, sugar, egg, and vanilla extract in a medium bowl. Set aside.

3. For the muffins, mix together the flour, sugar, cocoa, baking soda, and salt in a large bowl. In another bowl, stir together the sour cream, oil, melted butter, eggs, vanilla, and melted chocolate. Add the wet ingredients to the dry ingredients and stir until just combined.

4. Spoon the batter into the prepared pan and then carefully spoon the reserved cheesecake mixture over the chocolate batter in the prepared muffin cups and swirl slightly with a knife so the batter appears marbled. Sprinkle with almonds.

5. Bake until risen and golden, 20 to 25 minutes. Cool in the pan for 5 minutes, then turn out onto a wire rack. Serve warm or cold.

Cappuccino Muffins

Do not be tempted to substitute instant coffee for ground coffee. If possible, use a rich, dark roasted brand for the best flavor.

Makes 12

¾ cup/115 g self-rising flour
1¼ cups/185 g all-purpose flour
1 tbsp baking powder
½ tsp salt
⅔ cup/60 g unsweetened cocoa powder
½ cup/100 g packed brown sugar
2 tbsp finely ground coffee
6 tbsp butter, softened
1 cup/225 ml sour cream
1 cup/225 ml whipping cream
2 eggs, lightly beaten
Finely grated peel of 2 oranges
4 oz/125 g bittersweet chocolate,
   coarsely chopped

1. Preheat oven to 350°F/180°C. Grease a 12-cup muffin pan or line with muffin cups.

2. In a large bowl, mix the flours, baking powder, salt, and cocoa. Stir in the brown sugar and coffee.

3. In another bowl, beat the butter, sour cream, cream, and eggs. Add the wet ingredients to the dry ingredients along with the orange peel and chocolate and mix until just combined.

4. Spoon the batter evenly into the prepared pan and bake until risen, golden, and firm, 15 to 20 minutes. Cool in the pan for 10 minutes, then turn out onto a wire rack. Serve warm or cold.

Glazed Mocha Chocolate Chip Muffins

*The addition of a little espresso makes
these muffins quite sophisticated.*

Makes 12

2 cups/300 g self-rising flour
1 tsp baking powder
4 tbsp butter
Generous ⅓ cup/80 g sugar
Scant 1 cup/150g semisweet chocolate
   chips or chopped semisweet chocolate
2 eggs, lightly beaten
⅔ cup/150 ml milk
5 tbsp/75 ml fresh espresso

For the chocolate glaze:
2 tbsp butter
2 tbsp unsweetened cocoa powder
2 tbsp espresso
Scant 1¼ cups/150 g confectioners'
   sugar, sifted
½ tsp vanilla extract

1. Preheat the oven to 400°F/200°C. Grease a
12-cup muffin pan or line with muffin cups.

2. Mix the flour and baking powder in a
large bowl. Rub in the butter until the
mixture resembles fine breadcrumbs. Stir
in the sugar and chocolate. In a bowl, whisk
together the eggs, milk, and espresso, then
pour the mixture all at once into the dry
ingredients and mix until just blended.

3. Spoon the batter evenly into the prepared
pan and bake until well risen, golden, and
firm to the touch, 18 to 20 minutes. Cool in
the pan for 5 minutes, then turn out onto a
wire rack.

4. For the glaze, melt the butter in a small
pan over low heat. Add the cocoa and
espresso, stirring constantly until the
mixture thickens; do not boil. Remove from
the heat and slowly add the confectioners'
sugar and vanilla, beating until smooth. If
necessary, thin with a little hot water until
thin enough to drizzle over the cooled
muffins. Let stand for 30 minutes until set.

Chocolate Fudge Muffins

These muffins pack a real chocolate punch—not for the fainthearted.

Makes 12

5 oz/150 g semisweet chocolate,
   coarsely chopped
2 oz/50 g unsweetened chocolate,
   coarsely chopped
6 tbsp butter
2 cups/300 g all-purpose flour
¾ cup/150 g packed brown sugar
1 tsp baking soda
¼ tsp salt
¾ cup/175 ml sour cream
¼ cup/50 ml light corn syrup
1 egg, lightly beaten
1¼ tsp vanilla extract
Generous ½ cup/100 g semisweet
   chocolate chips

1. Preheat the oven to 400°F/200°C. Grease a 12-cup muffin pan or line with muffin cups.

2. Melt the semisweet chocolate, unsweetened chocolate, and butter together in a medium bowl set over a pan of barely simmering water, stirring occasionally until smooth. Cool slightly.

3. Mix the flour, brown sugar, baking soda, and salt in another bowl. In a small bowl, whisk the sour cream, corn syrup, egg, and vanilla, then fold into the chocolate mixture. Fold in the chocolate chips. Add the chocolate mixture to the dry ingredients, stirring until just combined.

4. Spoon the batter evenly into the prepared pan. Bake until well risen and firm, about 20 minutes. Cool in the pan for 5 minutes, then turn out onto a wire rack.

Chocolate Chip and Orange Muffins

*The orange peel adds a freshness here,
for those who find chocolate muffins a
little overwhelming.*

Makes 12

2 cups/300 g all-purpose flour
1 cup/200 g packed brown sugar
⅓ cup/35 g unsweetened cocoa powder
2 tsp baking soda
½ tsp salt
Generous ½ cup/100 g semisweet
  chocolate chips
1 cup/225 ml milk
6 tbsp butter or margarine, melted
2 eggs, lightly beaten
Finely grated peel of 1 orange

1. Preheat oven to 400°F/200°C. Grease a
12-cup muffin pan or line with muffin cups.

2. In a large bowl, mix together the flour,
brown sugar, cocoa, baking soda, salt, and
chocolate chips.

3. In another bowl, whisk together the milk,
butter, eggs, and orange peel until blended.
Add the wet ingredients to the dry
ingredients and mix until just combined.

4. Spoon the batter evenly into the
prepared pan and bake until well risen and
firm, 25 to 30 minutes. Cool in the pan for
5 minutes, then turn out onto a wire rack.
Serve warm or cold.

CHAPTER THREE

. . . .

Nuts 'n' Spices

Peanut Butter and Banana Muffins

Your favorite sandwich combination, in a muffin!

Makes 12

1½ cups/225 g all-purpose flour
1 cup/100 g rolled oats (instant
  or regular)
¼ cup/50 g packed brown sugar
1 tbsp baking powder
½ tsp salt
⅓ cup/100 g crunchy peanut butter
1 cup/225 ml milk
1 tbsp maple syrup
1 egg, lightly beaten
2 very ripe bananas, peeled and mashed
1 tbsp granulated sugar
1 tsp ground cinnamon

1. Preheat the oven to 400°F/200°C. Grease a 12-cup muffin pan or line with muffin cups.

2. In a large bowl, mix together the flour and the oats, then stir in the brown sugar. Add the baking powder and salt and mix again until well combined.

3. In another bowl, mix the peanut butter, milk, maple syrup, egg, and bananas until well blended. Add the wet ingredients to the dry ingredients all at once, stirring briefly until just combined.

4. Spoon the batter evenly into the prepared pan. Mix the sugar and cinnamon and sprinkle over the muffins. Bake until risen and golden, about 20 minutes. Cool in the pan for 10 minutes, then turn out onto a wire rack. Serve warm or cold.

Sweet Potato Muffins with Pecans and Cinnamon

The sweetness of the potato goes beautifully with the cinnamon, and the nuts add a welcome crunch.

Makes 12

1 large orange-fleshed sweet potato (yam)
½ cup/1 stick/125 g butter, softened
1 cup/225 g sugar
2 eggs, lightly beaten
2 cups/300 g all-purpose flour
2 tsp baking powder
¼ tsp salt
1 tsp ground cinnamon
½ tsp grated nutmeg
1 cup/225 ml milk
½ cup/65 g chopped pecans

1. Preheat oven to 400°F/200°C. Grease a 12-cup muffin pan or line with muffin cups.

2. Prick the sweet potato several times with a fork and place on a baking sheet at a high temperature in the oven. Bake until tender, 25 to 30 minutes. Remove from the oven and let stand until cool enough to handle.

3. When cool, cut the sweet potato in half and scoop out the flesh. Transfer to a small bowl and mash until smooth. You should have about 1 cup/225 g. Set aside.

4. In a large bowl, cream the butter and sugar. Beat in the eggs and sweet potatoes.

5. In another bowl, mix the flour, baking powder, salt, cinnamon, and nutmeg. Add to the butter mixture alternately with the milk, stirring just until combined. Fold in the pecans.

6. Spoon the batter evenly into the prepared pan and bake until risen and golden, 20 to 25 minutes. Cool in the pan for 10 minutes, then turn out onto a wire rack. Serve warm or cold.

Honey and Pistachio Muffins

This recipe is inspired by baklava, *the sweet and sticky Middle Eastern pastry flavored with nuts and honey. Use a scented honey for the best result.*

Makes 12

2 cups/300 g all-purpose flour
1 tbsp baking powder
½ tsp salt
1 tsp ground cinnamon
Pinch of ground cloves
3 tbsp chopped pistachios
3 tbsp chopped blanched almonds
½ cup/100 g packed brown sugar
4 tbsp honey
1 cup/225 ml milk
2 tbsp vegetable oil
2 eggs, lightly beaten

1. Preheat the oven to 400°F/200°C. Grease a 12-cup muffin pan or line with muffin cups.

2. Mix the flour, baking powder, salt, cinnamon, and cloves in a large bowl. Stir in 2 tablespoons of the pistachios, 2 tablespoons of the almonds, and the brown sugar.

3. In another bowl, mix 2 tablespoons of the honey with the milk, oil, and eggs. Add the wet ingredients to the dry ingredients all at once and stir briefly until just combined.

4. Spoon the batter evenly into the prepared pan. Sprinkle with the remaining nuts and bake until risen and golden, 18 to 20 minutes. Remove from the oven and drizzle with the remaining 2 tablespoons honey. Cool in the pan for 10 minutes, then turn out onto a wire rack. Best eaten warm.

Coffee Walnut Muffins

Makes 12

⅔ cup/100 g walnuts
Scant ¾ cup/1¼ sticks/150 g butter
⅔ cup/150 g sugar
3 egg whites
4 egg yolks
1 tsp vanilla extract
1 cup/150 g all-purpose flour
1 tsp baking powder

For the coffee frosting:
1½ tbsp milk
Small pat of butter
1 tbsp instant coffee granules
1½ cups/200 g confectioners' sugar, sifted
1 tsp vanilla extract

1. Preheat the oven to 350°F/180°C. Grease a 12-cup muffin pan or line with muffin cups.

2. Chop the walnuts finely in a food processor; do not allow them to become pasty. Set aside.

3. Melt the butter and sugar in a pan over low heat. Gently bring the mixture to a boil and cook for 2 minutes, stirring constantly. Be careful not to brown or burn the mixture. Let cool.

4. Beat the egg whites until stiff; set aside. Add the egg yolks to the cooled sugar-butter mixture, then stir in the chopped walnuts, vanilla, flour, and baking powder. Gently fold in the egg whites to make a soft, thick batter.

5. Spoon the batter evenly into the prepared pan and bake until firm and golden, 15 to 20 minutes. Cool in the pan for 10 minutes, then turn out onto a wire rack.

6. For the frosting, heat the milk, butter, and instant coffee in a small pan over low heat. Add the confectioners' sugar and vanilla and stir until smooth, adding a little more confectioners' sugar if necessary to make a spreading consistency. Spread the frosting on the cooled muffins.

Peanut Butter Muffins

For a pure, unadulterated peanut butter hit, try these mouth-watering muffins accompanied by a cold glass of milk.

Makes 12

2 cups/300 g all-purpose flour
1½ tsp baking powder
½ tsp salt
4 tbsp finely chopped unsalted,
  roasted peanuts
½ cup/100 g packed brown sugar
Scant ¾ cup/200 g smooth peanut butter
¾ cup/175 ml milk
2 tbsp vegetable oil
2 eggs, lightly beaten
1 tbsp demerara sugar

1. Preheat the oven to 375°F/190°C. Grease a 12-cup muffin pan or line with muffin cups.

2. In a large bowl, mix the flour, baking powder, and salt. Stir in 2 tablespoons of the chopped peanuts and the brown sugar. Add the peanut butter and rub in until the mixture resembles coarse breadcrumbs.

3. In another bowl mix the milk, oil, and eggs. Add the wet ingredients to the dry ingredients all at once and mix briefly until just combined.

4. Spoon the batter evenly into the prepared pan. Combine the remaining chopped peanuts and demerara sugar and sprinkle evenly over the muffins. Bake until risen and golden, 16 to 18 minutes. Cool in the pan for 10 minutes, then turn out onto a wire rack. Serve warm or cold.

Spiced Zucchini Muffins

Choose smaller, firm zucchini rather than larger specimens as they will be less watery and give a better end result.

Makes 12

2 cups/300 g wholewheat flour
½ cup/100 g packed brown sugar
1½ tbsp baking powder
½ tsp salt
1 tsp ground cinnamon
¾ cup/175 ml milk
2 eggs, lightly beaten
¼ cup/50 ml vegetable oil
¼ cup/50 ml honey
Generous ½ cup/120 g grated zucchini

1. Preheat the oven to 375°F/190°C. Grease a 12-cup muffin pan or line with muffin cups.

2. In a large bowl, mix the flour, brown sugar, baking powder, salt, and cinnamon.

3. In another bowl, mix the milk, eggs, oil, honey, and zucchini. Pour the wet ingredients into the dry ingredients all at once and mix until just combined.

4. Spoon the batter evenly into the prepared pan. Bake until risen and lightly browned, about 20 minutes. Cool in the pan for 10 minutes, then turn out onto a wire rack. Serve warm.

Jam-Filled Mini Muffins

You can also make 12 regular-sized muffins if you prefer a larger treat.

Makes 36

1⅔ cups/250 g self-rising flour
1 tsp baking powder
4 tbsp butter
⅓ cup/80 g sugar
2 eggs, lightly beaten
1 cup/225 ml milk
1 tsp vanilla extract
5 to 6 tbsp raspberry or strawberry jam

For the topping:
4 tbsp butter
1 tsp ground cinnamon
¼ cup/50 g sugar

1. Preheat the oven to 400°F/200°C. Grease three 12-cup mini-muffin pans or line with mini-muffin cups.

2. In a large bowl, mix the flour and baking powder. Rub in the butter until the mixture resembles fine breadcrumbs. Stir in the sugar.

3. In a small bowl, whisk together the eggs, milk, and vanilla, then pour the mixture all at once into the dry ingredients and mix briefly until just blended.

4. Put a small spoonful of the mixture into each prepared muffin cup. Add about ½ teaspoon of jam to each, then top with the remaining muffin batter. Bake until well risen, golden, and firm to the touch, 8 to 10 minutes. Cool in the pan for a few minutes, then turn out onto a wire rack.

5. For the topping, melt the butter over low heat. In a small bowl, mix the cinnamon and sugar. Brush each mini muffin all over with a little melted butter, then roll in the cinnamon sugar. Set aside to cool. Serve warm or cold.

Butter Tart Muffins with Raisins and Walnuts

These muffins are everything a butter tart should be—gooey and buttery. Leave out the nuts and raisins if you prefer.

Makes 12

1⅓ cups/200 g raisins
¾ cup/175 g sugar
½ cup/1 stick/125 g butter
½ cup/125 ml milk
1 tsp vanilla or rum extract
2 eggs, lightly beaten
2 cups/300 g all-purpose flour
2 tsp baking powder
1 tsp baking soda
Pinch of salt
½ cup/65 g walnuts, chopped
¼ cup/50 ml corn syrup

1. Preheat the oven to 375°F/190°C. Grease a 12-cup muffin pan or line with muffin cups.

2. Combine the raisins, sugar, butter, milk, and extract in a large pan. Place over medium heat and cook, stirring almost constantly, until mixture is hot and the sugar has melted. Bring just to a simmer, then remove from the heat. Let cool for 10 minutes, then whisk in the eggs. Let cool until just warm.

3. In a large bowl, mix the flour, baking powder, baking soda, and salt. Make a well in the center and pour in the raisin mixture, stirring until just combined. Stir in the walnuts until just mixed. Spoon the batter evenly into the prepared pan. Bake until risen and golden, 15 to 17 minutes.

4. Remove from the oven and immediately pour about 1 teaspoon corn syrup over the top of each muffin. Cool for 10 minutes in the pan, then turn out onto a wire rack. Serve warm or cold.

Cinnamon and Pecan Muffins

If you can't find buttermilk anywhere, mix 1 teaspoon white vinegar into ¾ cup/175 ml of milk and leave at room temperature for 1 hour, until slightly curdled.

Makes 12

2 cups/300 g all-purpose flour
1 tsp baking powder
1 tsp baking soda
Pinch of salt
½ cup/1 stick/125 g butter, softened
Generous ¾ cup/175 g sugar
2 eggs, lightly beaten
1 tsp vanilla extract
¾ cup/175 ml buttermilk
⅜ cup/75 g packed brown sugar
1 tsp ground cinnamon
½ cup/65 g pecans, coarsely chopped

1. Preheat the oven to 375°F/190°C. Grease a 12-cup muffin pan or line with muffin cups.

2. In a large bowl, mix the flour, baking powder, baking soda, and salt.

3. In another bowl, cream together the butter and sugar until light and fluffy. Gradually beat in the eggs and vanilla. Stir in the buttermilk.

4. Add the wet ingredients to the dry ingredients all at once and mix briefly until only just blended.

5. In a small bowl, mix the brown sugar, cinnamon, and pecans.

6. Spoon half the batter evenly into the prepared pan and sprinkle with half the nut mixture. Repeat with the remaining batter and nut mixture, gently pressing the nuts into the batter with the back of a spoon or a rubber spatula. Bake until well risen and firm, 20 to 25 minutes. Cool in the pan for 10 minutes, then turn out onto a wire rack to cool. Serve warm or cold.

CHAPTER FOUR

. . . .

Savory Muffins

Bacon Corn Muffins

These are a variation on the usual corn muffin. They're great for breakfast or for a light lunch with a little green salad on the side.

Makes 12

8 oz/225 g sliced bacon
1 small onion, finely chopped
1 cup/150 g all-purpose flour
1¼ cups/170 g fine cornmeal
2 tbsp sugar
4 tsp baking powder
½ tsp salt
Scant 1 cup/200 g cream-style corn
½ cup/125 ml milk
1 egg, lightly beaten

1. Preheat the oven to 425°F/220°C. Grease a 12-cup muffin pan or line with muffin cups.

2. Cook the bacon, either under the broiler or in a large frying pan, until crisp. Drain well on paper towels. Add the onion to the same pan and sauté until soft and lightly golden, 5 to 7 minutes. Crumble or chop the bacon into small pieces and set aside with the onion. Reserve about ¼ cup/50 ml of the bacon drippings.

3. In a medium bowl, mix the flour, cornmeal, sugar, baking powder, and salt.

4. In another bowl, beat the corn, milk, egg, and reserved bacon drippings. Add the corn mixture to the flour mixture and mix briefly until just combined. Fold in the reserved bacon and onion.

5. Spoon evenly into the prepared pan and bake until golden, 15 to 20 minutes. Carefully remove the muffins from the pan Best served warm from the oven.

Cajun Spiced Corn Muffins

These smell wonderful as they are baking and are a great accompaniment to any Cajun-style stew or fish dish.

Makes 12

1¼ cups/170 g fine cornmeal
1 cup/150 g all-purpose flour
1 tbsp sugar
1 tbsp baking powder
1 tsp salt
½ tsp baking soda
½ tsp Cajun spice mix
¾ cup/175 ml buttermilk
2 eggs, lightly beaten
½ cup/85 g frozen corn
¼ cup finely chopped green onions (about 2)
2 tbsp vegetable oil
¼ tsp hot pepper sauce (or to taste)

1. Preheat the oven to 425°F/220°C. Grease a 12-cup muffin pan or line with muffin cups.

2. In a large bowl, mix the cornmeal, flour, sugar, baking powder, salt, baking soda, and Cajun spice mix.

3. In another bowl, mix the buttermilk, eggs, corn, green onions, oil, and hot pepper sauce. Add the wet ingredients to the dry ingredients all at once and mix briefly until just combined.

4. Spoon evenly into the prepared pan and bake until well risen and golden, 18 to 20 minutes. Cool in the pan for 5 minutes then turn out onto a wire rack. Serve warm.

Cheesy Double Corn Muffins

*These muffins are fabulous served
with a hot bowl of spicy chili or fresh
tomato soup.*

Makes 12

¾ cup/125 g all-purpose flour
1¼ cups/170 g fine cornmeal
1 tsp baking soda
1 tsp baking powder
2 tsp salt
¼ cup/50 g vegetable shortening
¾ cup/75 g grated cheddar cheese
2 eggs, lightly beaten
1 cup/225 ml milk
Scant 1 cup/200 g canned
  cream-style corn

1. Preheat the oven to 425°F/220°C.
Grease a 12-cup muffin pan or line with
muffin cups.

2. In a large bowl, mix the flour, cornmeal,
baking soda, baking powder, and salt. Add
the shortening and rub in until the mixture
resembles coarse breadcrumbs. Stir in the
grated cheese.

3. In another bowl, mix the eggs and milk.
Add to the dry ingredients along with
the creamed corn and stir briefly until
just combined.

4. Spoon evenly into the prepared pan
and bake until risen and golden, 25 to
30 minutes. Cool in the pan for 10 minutes
before serving. These are best served on
the day they are baked, warm from the
oven if possible.

Plantain and Herb Muffins

Plantains can be eaten at every stage of ripeness but must be cooked. When green, their flavor and texture is akin to potato; when ripe (and black), they are more similar to the bananas they resemble, becoming sweet and soft.

Makes 12

2 cups/300 g all-purpose flour
1 tbsp baking powder
1 tsp baking soda
1 tsp salt
1 tbsp fresh thyme leaves
1 tbsp chopped fresh chives
1 tbsp chopped fresh parsley
1 clove garlic, crushed
¾ cup/175 ml plain yogurt
⅔ cup/150 ml milk
2 eggs, lightly beaten
2 tbsp vegetable oil
1 tbsp prepared horseradish
1 large green plantain, grated

1. Preheat the oven to 400°F/200°C. Grease a 12-cup muffin pan or line with muffin cups.

2. Mix the flour, baking powder, baking soda, and salt in a large bowl. Add the thyme, chives, parsley, and garlic and mix well.

3. In another bowl, mix the yogurt, milk, eggs, and oil. Add the wet ingredients to the dry ingredients all at once with the horseradish and plantain, and mix briefly until just combined.

4. Spoon the batter evenly into the prepared pan and bake until risen and golden, 20 to 25 minutes. Cool in the pan for 10 minutes, then turn out onto a wire rack to cool. Serve warm or cold.

Chive and Cottage Cheese Muffins

These savory muffins would make a very nice light lunch with some soup and perhaps a side salad.

Makes 12

2 cups/300 g self-rising flour
½ tsp baking powder
½ tsp baking soda
½ tsp salt
4 tbsp butter, softened
¼ cup/50 g packed brown sugar
1 egg, lightly beaten
Generous 1 cup/250 g cottage cheese
¼ cup/50 ml skim milk
3 tbsp chopped fresh chives

1. Preheat the oven to 375°F/190°C. Grease a 12-cup muffin pan or line with muffin cups.

2. Mix the flour, baking powder, baking soda, and salt in a large bowl. In another bowl, cream the butter and brown sugar. Beat in the egg. Add the cottage cheese and milk and mix until smooth. Add to the dry ingredients until just combined.

3. Spoon the batter into the prepared pan and bake until risen and golden, about 20 minutes. Cool in the pan for 10 minutes, then turn out onto a wire rack.

Sausage Cheese Muffins

Use the best quality sausages you can afford, as they are the predominant flavor in these muffins.

Makes 12

8 oz/225 g ground pork sausage
1 small onion, grated
2 cups/300 g all-purpose flour
2 tbsp sugar
1 tbsp baking powder
¼ tsp salt
¾ cup/175 ml milk
1 large egg, lightly beaten
4 tbsp butter, melted
½ cup/50 g grated cheddar cheese

1. Preheat the oven to 375°F/190°C. Grease a 12-cup muffin pan or line with muffin cups.

2. In a large frying pan, cook the sausage meat over high heat until cooked through and golden, 8 to 10 minutes, breaking up the meat with a wooden spoon. Drain on paper towels and set aside. Add the onion to the pan and cook until softened, 3 to 4 minutes. Drain and set aside.

3. Mix together the flour, sugar, baking powder, and salt in a large bowl. In another bowl, mix the milk, egg, and melted butter. Add to the dry ingredients all at once along with the cheese, sausage, and onion. Mix briefly until just combined.

4. Spoon the batter into the prepared muffin pan and bake until well risen and golden, about 20 minutes. Cool in the pan for 10 minutes, then turn out onto a wire rack. These are best served warm.

Beer and Onion Muffins

This unlikely combination works really well—the perfect partner to an afternoon watching the soccer or a lazy summer's day picnic.

Makes 12

2 cups/300 g all-purpose flour
2 tbsp sugar
1 tbsp baking powder
1 tsp salt
½ tsp ground black pepper
½ tsp garlic powder
1 cup/225 ml beer, allowed to go flat
    and at room temperature
½ cup/125 ml vegetable oil
1 egg, lightly beaten
1 small onion, grated
1 tbsp fresh thyme leaves

1. Preheat the oven to 400°F/200°C. Grease a 12-cup muffin pan or line with muffin cups.

2. Mix the flour, sugar, baking powder, salt, pepper, and garlic powder in a large bowl.

3. In another bowl, whisk together the beer, oil, egg, onion, and thyme. Add the wet ingredients to the dry ingredients, all at once, and mix until just combined.

4. Spoon the batter into the prepared pan and bake until risen and golden, about 25 minutes. Cool for 10 minutes in the pan, then turn out onto a wire rack. Serve immediately.

Onion and Cheese Muffins

These are deeply savory muffins that go well with soups or stews.

Makes 12

4 tbsp vegetable oil
1 large onion, finely sliced
2 cups/300 g all-purpose flour
¾ cup/75 g shredded, sharp
  cheddar cheese
1 tbsp baking powder
1 tsp onion salt
1 cup/225 ml milk
2 large eggs, lightly beaten

1. Preheat the oven to 350°F/180°C. Grease a 12-cup muffin pan or line with muffin cups.

2. Heat 1 tablespoon of the oil in a frying pan, add the onion and cook over medium heat until crisp and golden, 8 to 10 minutes. Drain on paper towels. When cool enough to handle, crumble or chop coarsely.

3. In a large bowl, mix the flour, fried onion, cheddar cheese, baking powder, and onion salt. In another bowl, mix the milk, eggs, and remaining oil. Add the wet ingredients to the dry ingredients all at once, and mix briefly until just combined.

4. Spoon the batter evenly into the prepared pan. Bake until risen and golden, 15 to 18 minutes. Cool in the pan for 10 minutes before turning out onto a wire rack. Serve warm.

Pizza Muffins

All the great flavors of a pizza, but more compact.

Makes 12

⅓ cup/75 ml olive oil
Generous 1 cup/65 g sliced mushrooms
¾ cup/50 g chopped pepperoni sausage
½ cup/85 g chopped ham
1 medium onion, grated
1⅓ cups/150 g grated mozzarella cheese
⅓ cup/75 g chopped sun-dried tomatoes,
   drained if in oil
1 tbsp minced fresh garlic
1 tsp dried oregano
1 tbsp chopped fresh basil
2 eggs, lightly beaten
½ cup/125 ml milk
2 cups/300 g all-purpose flour
1 tbsp baking powder
Salt and freshly ground black pepper

1. Preheat the oven to 375°F/190°C. Grease a 12-cup muffin pan or line with muffin cups.

2. Heat 1½ tablespoons of the oil in a large frying pan. Add the mushrooms and cook over high heat, about 5 minutes, turning often, until the mushrooms are golden and tender. Set aside to cool.

3. In a large bowl, combine the pepperoni, ham, onion, cheese, tomatoes, garlic, oregano, basil, and cooled mushrooms.

4. In another bowl, blend the eggs, milk, and remaining olive oil. Add to the pepperoni mixture. Season well with salt and pepper.

5. In another bowl, mix the flour and baking powder. Add to the wet ingredients and mix briefly until just combined.

6. Spoon the batter into the prepared pan and bake until risen and lightly golden, 20 to 25 minutes. Cool in the pan for 10 minutes before turning out onto a wire rack. These are best served warm.

Pumpkin, Cheese, and Pumpkin Seed Muffins

Crunchy and cheesy, these muffins are perfect for a buffet.

Makes 12

2 cups/300 g all-purpose flour
1 tbsp baking powder
1 tsp baking soda
1 tsp salt
1 cup/100 g coarsely diced firm
    goat cheese
4 tbsp toasted pumpkin seeds
Scant 1 cup/200 g pumpkin puree,
    canned or fresh
¾ cup/175 ml plain yogurt
2 eggs, lightly beaten
2 tbsp vegetable oil

1. Preheat the oven to 400°F/200°C. Grease a 12-cup muffin pan or line with muffin cups.

2. Mix the flour, baking powder, baking soda, and salt in a large bowl. Stir in the goat cheese. Coarsely chop 2 tablespoons of the pumpkin seeds and set aside the remainder. Stir the chopped pumpkin seeds into the flour mixture.

3. In another bowl, whisk together the pumpkin puree, yogurt, eggs, and oil. Add the wet ingredients to the dry ingredients all at once, and mix briefly until just combined.

4. Spoon the batter into the prepared pan and sprinkle with the remaining pumpkin seeds. Bake until risen and golden, 20 to 25 minutes. Cool in the pan for 10 minutes, then turn out onto a wire rack. Serve warm.

Sweet Potato, Roasted Chili, and Feta Muffins

Makes 12

1 medium orange-fleshed sweet potato
  (yam)
1 hot red chili
2 cups/300 g all-purpose flour
1 tbsp baking powder
½ tsp salt
1 garlic clove, crushed
1 tsp cumin seeds, toasted, lightly crushed
1 tbsp chopped fresh basil
2 eggs, lightly beaten
1 cup/225 ml milk
¼ cup/50 ml olive oil, plus extra
  for brushing
¾ cup/75 g crumbled feta cheese

1. Preheat the oven to 400°F/200°C. Grease a 12-cup muffin pan or line with muffin cups.

2. Bake the sweet potato in the preheated oven until tender, about 30 minutes. Let stand until cool enough to handle, then scoop out the flesh and mash. Set aside.

3. Brush the chili with a little olive oil and place under the broiler or over an open flame until scorched and blackened. Put into a small plastic bag until cool enough to handle. Peel the chili, removing all the blackened skin. Slit the chili open and remove the stem, seeds, and membranes. Chop the flesh finely. Set aside.

4. Mix the flour, baking powder, and salt in a large bowl. Stir in the garlic, cumin, and basil.

5. In another bowl, beat the eggs with the milk, olive oil, and sweet potato. Add to the dry ingredients all at once along with the chopped chili. Fold in the crumbled feta, mixing until only just combined.

6. Spoon the batter into the prepared muffin pan and bake until well risen and golden, 20 to 25 minutes. Cool in the pan for 10 minutes, then turn out onto a wire rack to cool. These are best eaten warm.

Smoked Bacon and Blue Cheese Muffins

It's very important to drain the bacon well after frying so that it remains crisp and tasty.

Makes 12

8 oz/225 g bacon
2 cups/300 g all-purpose flour
1 tbsp baking powder
½ tsp salt
Generous ⅓ cup/80 g sugar
1 egg, lightly beaten
⅓ cup/85 ml water
¾ cup/175 ml milk
About 10 fresh basil leaves, finely chopped
¾ cup/75 g crumbled blue cheese
½ cup/65 g chopped walnuts

1. Preheat the oven to 350°F/180°C. Grease a 12-cup muffin pan or line with muffin cups.

2. Fry the bacon in a large frying pan until crisp. Drain on paper towels, reserving about ⅓ cup drippings (or substitute vegetable oil). Crumble the bacon and set aside.

3. In a large bowl, mix the flour, baking powder, salt, and sugar.

4. In another bowl, mix the reserved bacon fat or oil, egg, water, and milk. Add the wet ingredients to the dry ingredients all at once along with the bacon, basil, blue cheese, and walnuts and mix briefly until just combined.

5. Spoon the batter into the prepared pan and bake until risen and golden, 20 to 25 minutes. Cool in the pan for 10 minutes, then turn out onto a wire rack. Serve warm.

Glossary

The following culinary terms will provide useful guidelines for international readers.

U.S.	British	U.S.	British
All-purpose flour	Plain flour	Molasses	Black treacle
Baking soda	Bicarbonate of soda	Packed brown sugar	Muscovado sugar
Beat	Whisk	Pan	Tin
Cornstarch	Cornflour	Peel	Zest
Confectioners' sugar	Icing sugar	Plastic wrap	Cling film
Extract	Essence	Semisweet chocolate	Plain chocolate
Golden raisins	Sultanas	Shredded coconut	Desiccated coconut
Graham crackers	Digestive biscuits	Sugar	Caster sugar
Light corn syrup	Golden syrup	Vanilla bean	Vanilla pod
Light cream	Single cream	Wholewheat flour	Wholemeal flour

Picture Credits

Index